To my grandsons — with much love

Published by C.R. Gibson®
C. R. Gibson® is a registered trademark of Thomas Nelson, Inc., Nashville, Tennessee 37214
Design by Anderson Thomas Design, Nashville, Tennessee.
Cover Photography © 1999 Russ Harrington

Printed in Mexico

ISBN 0-7667-6660-8
GB4162

From

Mother

with

Love

For My Son

by Evelyn Borthwick

It's hard to tell a grownup son
How much he means to me;
But none the less, it's time I did,
For I want him to see.
So let's begin by taking a journey to the past,
A journey filled with memories —
Memories that last.
And let me take you back in time,
A time that just flew by;
A time I wish could have stood still,
As I look back and sigh.
So join me on this journey,
Of laughter, love and fun;
And know how much I love you,
My own, my darling son.

When my wish was granted
And you were on the way,
My heart was filled with happiness,
I knew not what to say.
That overwhelming feeling,
Complete and utter joy;
And how I longed that I would have
A darling little boy.
And all that I could think of,
And all that I could see,
Was one sweet tiny angel —
Would he look like dad or me?
I kept myself so healthy —
Eating things I should,
Giving you a start in life,
The best way that I could.

I set off on my journey,
With great anticipation —
Longing for this miracle,
God's very own creation.
And when I heard my doctor say,
"You have a little boy,"
I thought my heart would burst with pride,
That feeling of such joy.
And as I held you in my arms,
I promised then and there,
That always I'd protect you
With tender loving care.
And as I gently kissed you,
And held you to my heart,
I knew that this, for you and me,
Was just the very start.

I watched you while you slept,
I couldn't leave your side;
You'd stir and stretch and look at me,
Your eyes now open wide.
I'd pick you up, and talk to you,
Oh how you made me smile!
And all that I would want to do
Was stay with you awhile.
I simply wanted you to know
I couldn't love you more;
And wanted you to always feel
Contented and secure.
"Sweet little boy, I love you,"
I'd whisper in your ear;
"And just as long as I am close,
There's nothing you need fear."

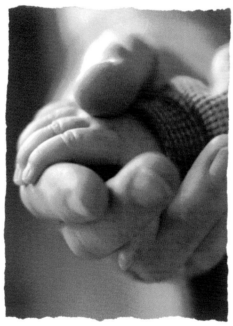

You seemed to grow so quickly;
The time went really fast.
You're not a tiny baby,
But a little boy at last.
You smile, you coo, you chatter,
In your own special way;
And I'm right there beside you,
As you sit and play.
You loved our time together,
I'm sure, as much as me;
And often you would do your best
To crawl onto my knee.
And sometimes you'd get angry,
And just a little weepy;
So I would tuck you in your bed,
'Cause I knew that you were sleepy.

Sometimes I really worried,
Those times you couldn't sleep;
And quietly I'd tiptoe —
Into your room I'd creep.
Your runny nose and watery eyes,
Filled with salty tears;
I'd pick you up and cuddle you,
And hope to ease your fears.
Yes, teething sure was painful —
Those sleepless nights we had;
And I would do my very best
To make you feel less sad.
Then I would tuck you back in bed,
Kissing you good night;
I'd creep out very softly
As I turned off your light.

You've become very active,
Crawling here and there.
Fingers always busy,
Tugging at my hair.
Opening all my cupboards,
Sorting pots and pans;
Getting into mischief,
With busy little hands.
It's me that gets frustrated,
And yet I have to smile;
I sit there in your corner
And stay with you awhile.
The joy to hear you laughing,
To see you have such fun;
No wonder I adore you,
My precious little son.

You were so excited
When Christmas came around;
The sights, they overwhelmed you,
You uttered not a sound.
The lights that blinked so brightly
And danced upon the tree;
The brightly packaged parcels
Were all that you could see.
I'd take you to the window
So you could watch it snow;
Falling down so softly,
It was really quite a show.
And then you'd laugh and giggle,
It gave me so much pleasure;
Oh sweetheart, I adored you,
You were my little treasure.

So now your first year's over
And didn't it go fast?
Those baby days and baby ways,
I wanted them to last.
When you saw your birthday cake
You clapped your hands with glee;
Once again, you toddle 'round
And climb onto my knee.
That day was very special,
Those photographs I took;
To treasure them forever
And paste them in a book.
So that when you are older,
You will surely see;
What a happy day that was,
Just for you and me.

That second year went quickly,
You grew and learned each day;
You loved your books, you loved your toys,
I loved to watch you play.
You're getting independent,
You want to show me how
You can tell the difference
"That horse is not a cow!"
You want to do it by yourself —
Teeth and toilet too,
Buttons, snaps on clothing —
Tie laces on your shoe.
And when you get frustrated
And give up in despair;
You come to me because you know,
For you I'm always there.

You woke up so excited,
For your first day of school;
You sat to eat your breakfast,
This was to be the rule.
You brushed your hair
And brushed your teeth
And waited by the gate.
You watched out for the school bus,
You hoped he'd not be late.
I felt a tiny tug of pain —
I guess because you're growing.
My eyes were filled with glistening tears,
I hoped that they weren't showing.
And as the bus pulled up,
And you waved me on your way,
I knew that this, for sure,
Would be a very special day.

Those fun days you had
With your friends as you'd play,
When time came for supper,
I'd invite them to stay.
Your fondness for spiders,
For frogs and for worms;
And all I could think of was
Hands filled with germs!
You loved the great outdoors
With so much to find;
You loved all the animals,
To them you were kind.
Yes, you loved all those things
That you found in the wild;
You sure were a curious,
Inquisitive child!

Those awful childhood ailments,
Like chicken pox and mumps,
Made you very grumpy
And left you in the dumps.
You didn't like the fact
You had to rest in bed;
You didn't want to hear me
No matter what I said.
I'd bring you little presents,
And read to you a story;
And when I brought you ice cream,
You were in your glory.
Then soon you felt much better,
Your friends popped in to say,
"Can we stay here with you?
Would you like to play?"

The weekends were our favorite;
We'd laze about and talk.
And if the day was sunny,
We'd go out for a walk.
We'd come home at our leisure,
And have a bite to eat;
Something very special,
A pleasant little treat.
You'd tell me funny stories,
Making silly faces —
Of far off lands, and dragons,
Found in magic places.
You made those times so special,
I wanted them to last;
But no, I couldn't stop them,
They just flew by too fast.

You sometimes liked to help me
In the kitchen when I'd cook,
And often you would lift the lids
And in the pots you'd look.
You'd tell me of your favorites —
Those very special dishes;
And I'd be happy to comply,
And grant you all your wishes.
We'd sit and eat together,
You'd tell me it was yummy;
And how you made me laugh,
Rubbing your full tummy.
Then I would do the dishes,
And you'd put them away;
You'd hug me and say,
"Thanks, Mom,"
And off you'd go and play.

I remember the first time
When you told me, "No!"
You made me quite angry, it upset me so.
I guess you were testing me,
Making it clear,
That you had some rights too —
So what was my fear?
I knew I could trust you,
For most of the time;
And speaking your own mind
Was surely no crime.
And if I had fears
Your choice was a mistake,
I had to believe
It was still yours to make.

There were times that you would lie to me,
And not tell me the truth;
But quickly you would realize
That this mom was a sleuth.
You had to learn real quickly
That this was not accepted;
And promises you made to me
Were meant to be respected.
I hated confrontations,
I didn't like to fight;
And later, when we cleared the air,
You saw that I was right.
You'd tell me you were sorry,
As I dried your tears away;
And resume talking quietly,
And start a brand new day.

You came to my room
And you looked such a sight,
And told me so sadly,
You'd been in a fight.
Your shirt and your jeans
And your shoes were so muddy,
Your face was all scratched
And your nose was all bloody.
And no matter how much
I'd strongly insist
For some explanation,
You'd firmly resist.
So I ran you a hot bath
To help you relax,
I knew that when ready,
You'd give me the facts.

From grade school to high school —
Oh my, how you've grown.
And now your soft voice
Has a much stronger tone.
You're mad about sports,
You're involved in them all;
You go with your friends —
They just have to call.
And I'm always happy,
And don't really mind,
To give you a lift
When you're stuck for a ride.
I'm happy to help
In the things that you do;
I wish those days back again —
My how time flew.

Sometimes we'd go off shopping,
Just the two of us;
We'd walk a little distance,
Waiting for our bus.
We'd gaze in all the windows,
Eat cookies filled with swirls;
And sometimes I would catch you
Smiling at the girls.
Oh my, how you are growing,
Time's flying oh so fast;
I wished that I could stop it —
I longed for this to last.
I realize quite quickly
You're not a little boy;
I can't explain my feeling —
But you fill my heart with joy.

I remember so well
When you first dated girls;
With short hair, with long hair,
With straight and with curls.
I also remember your first sad
Heartache;
You felt deep inside,
That it surely would break.
And I reassured you,
That this pain would go;
It happens to all of us,
Believe me, I know.
And one day the right girl
Will stay by your side;
You'll know it feels right
By that feeling of pride.

I loved those discussions —
The opinions you had;
And if I'd debate them,
You'd pretend to be mad.
You're strong and you're confident,
You have your own views;
And you're right to believe
In whatever you choose.
I'm so proud of the way
You defend what seems good;
It's the way that I taught you,
I agree that you should.
And just for the record,
In case you don't know,
I'm so proud that you're mine,
And I do love you so.

Gone are the scraped knees,
Those rough times you had;
And to tell you the truth,
I must say that I'm glad.
You fuss over clothes,
And you fuss over hair;
You like to be "trendy"
To show that you care.
And sometimes you'd ask me,
"Mom, what do you think?"
I'd smile at the sales clerk,
And she'd give me a wink.
No longer a child,
I see looking my way;
But now he's a young man,
Who grows day by day.

*M*any things you'd long for,
Like any other boy;
And earning your own money
Filled you with great joy.
Helping friends and neighbors,
Doing all you could —
Saving as you went along
Because you thought you should.
And you were so excited,
When you purchased your own bike;
Just in time to go with friends,
On a country hike.
And how it gave you pleasure
When you'd buy me a treat;
You really had a heart of gold,
You were so very sweet.

It was hard to decide
Which career you would take;
You had to be so sure
And to make no mistake.
You thought about options
With serious views;
You knew I'd support you,
I'd help you to choose.
You had goals and aspirations,
As I did for you;
And I know you'd reach them,
And you knew it too.
To earn well and enjoy life
Was your major dream;
These dreams were realistic —
So it would seem.

Time flew on by,
You became more mature;
We two were such good friends,
Of that we were sure.
You shared with me secrets,
Of plans and of schemes;
I share with you my fears,
My hopes and my dreams.
We always had time
For each other, that's true;
And how you could sense
When I sometimes felt blue.
How quickly you'd cheer me
In your own special way;
You'd make me forget,
That I'd had a bad day.

You studied for hours,
In your room through the night;
I'd ask you to "stop now,"
And turn off the light.
"Not yet," you would answer,
"Please, Mom, go to bed…"
And you'd just keep working,
No matter what I said.
I'd go to the kitchen,
And bring you a hot drink;
You laughed and said,
"Thanks Mom, it helps me to think."
I'm glad that you're serious
In these things you do;
And once more I sit back,
Oh my how time flew.

So hard work and hard play,
Was your way to live;
With all of your being,
With all you could give.
You dated some nice girls,
And broke a few hearts;
I knew this was normal,
Yes, that's how it starts.
And how I remember
That special girl you dated;
How happy you both were,
Completely elated.
Yet when it was over,
You missed not a beat;
To go out with your friends,
The next girl to meet!

How proud I am to tell you
What fun I've had with you;
And what a handsome gentle man
That you have turned out to.
And how you also make me feel
So special and secure;
Showing me in many ways,
How could I ask for more?
I'm such a lucky Mom
To have a son like you;
A very special bond,
You have to know it's true.
I only wish that time
Will keep us close together;
And know that in my heart
You will stay forever.

Well, those are all my memories
I wanted you to share;
These warm and loving feelings,
To tell you how I care.
I look at all the photographs
When you were just a boy;
And how they stir up feelings
Of complete and total joy.
Please keep these words I offer you,
They tell you of our life;
And one day, if God wills it,
You can share them with your wife.
I pray your life will always be
Filled with love and laughter;
And for you, my son, my heartfelt love —
Now and ever after.